the encouraging Rainbow coloring book

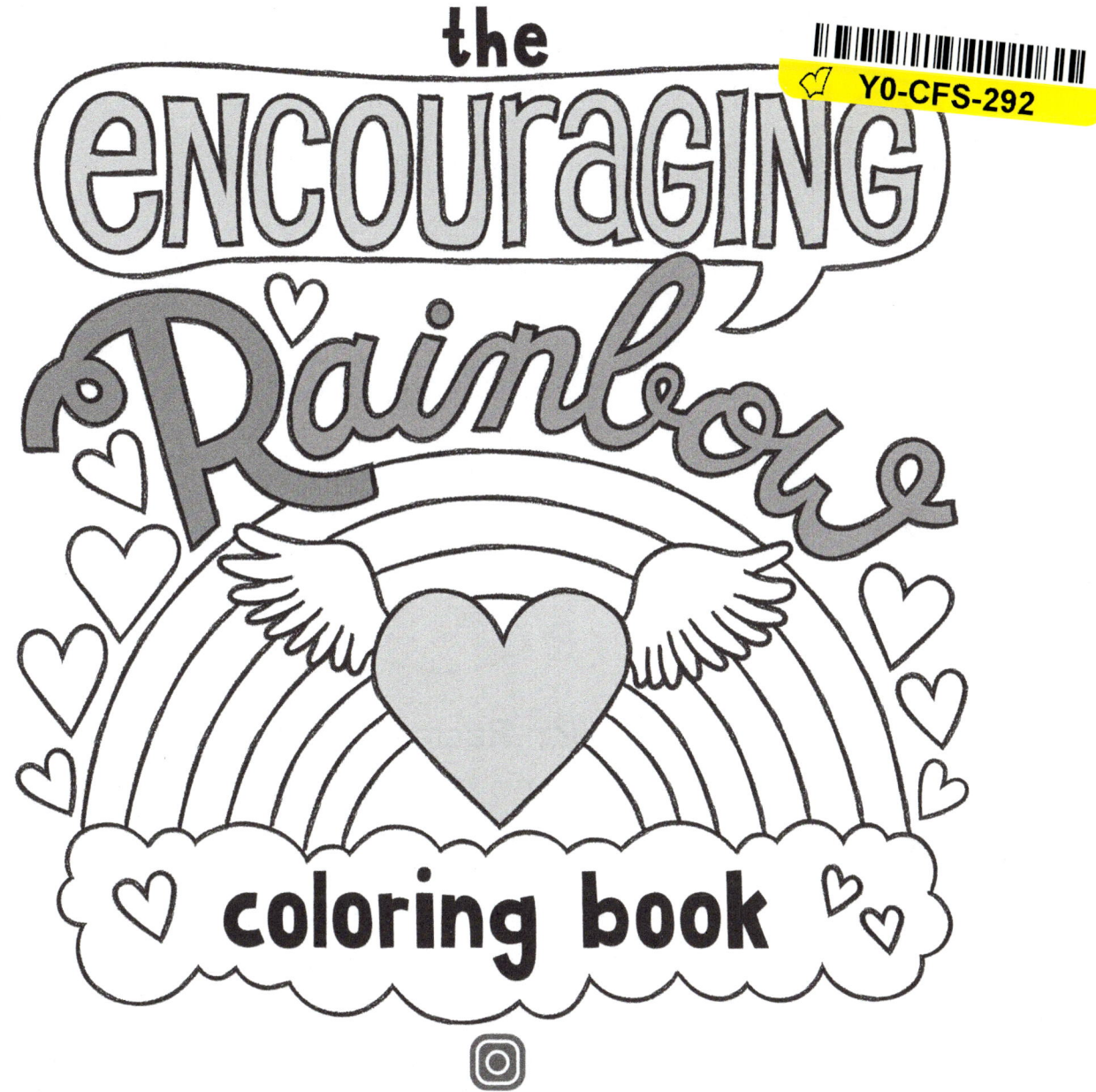

instagram: @jenracinecoloring

facebook.com/jenracinecoloring

www.jenracine.com

Find all the **Jen Racine** coloring books
in online bookstores.

Find coloring pages on **Etsy**:
JenRacineColoring

Copyright © 2020 by Eclectic Esquire Media LLC

ISBN: 978-1-951728-50-2

No part of this publication may be reproduced, distributed or transmitted in any form or by any means, without the prior written permission of the publisher, except in the case of brief quotations embodied in critical reviews and certain other noncommerical uses permitted by copyright law.

STAY COLORFUL

I Believe in me

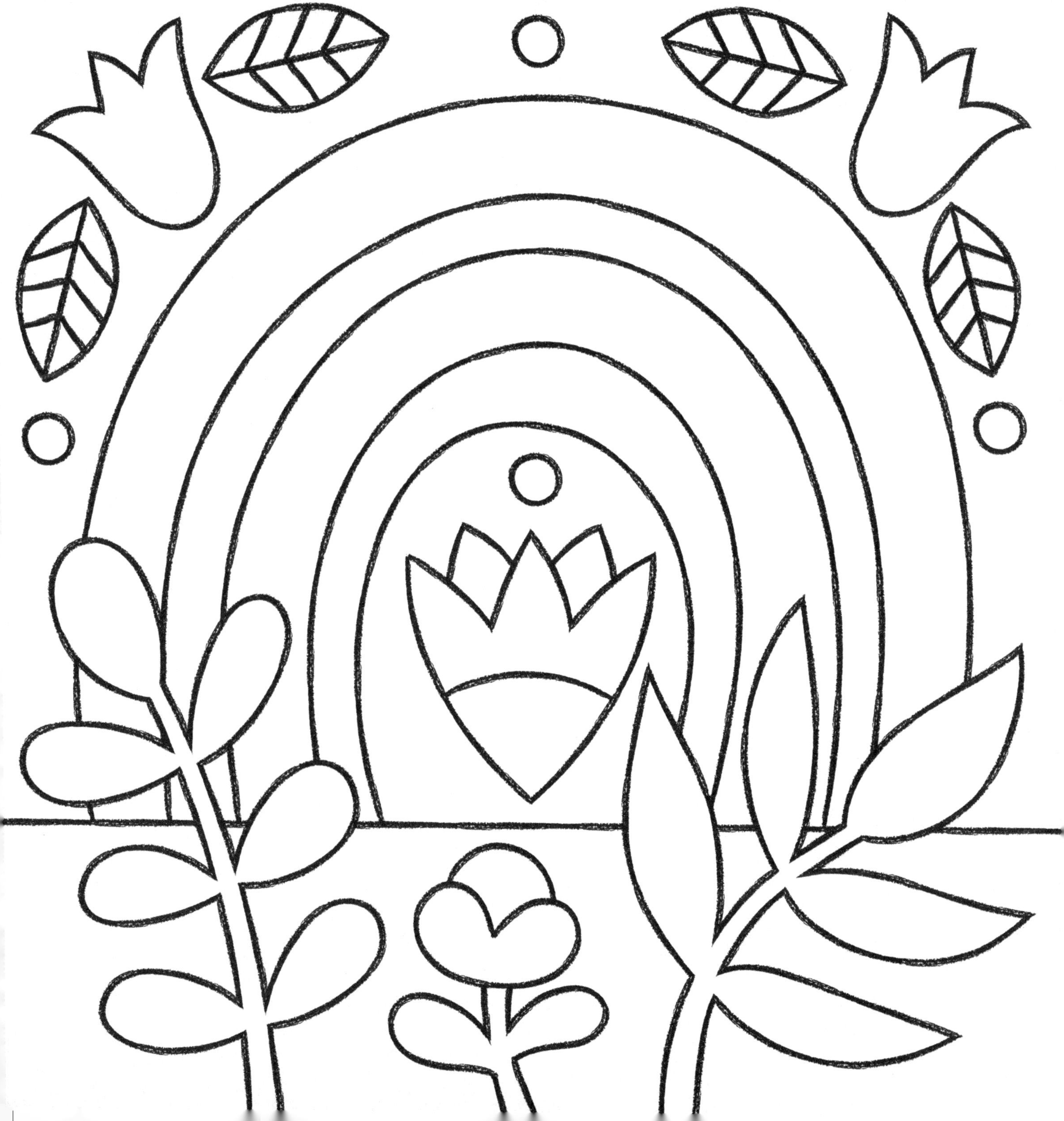

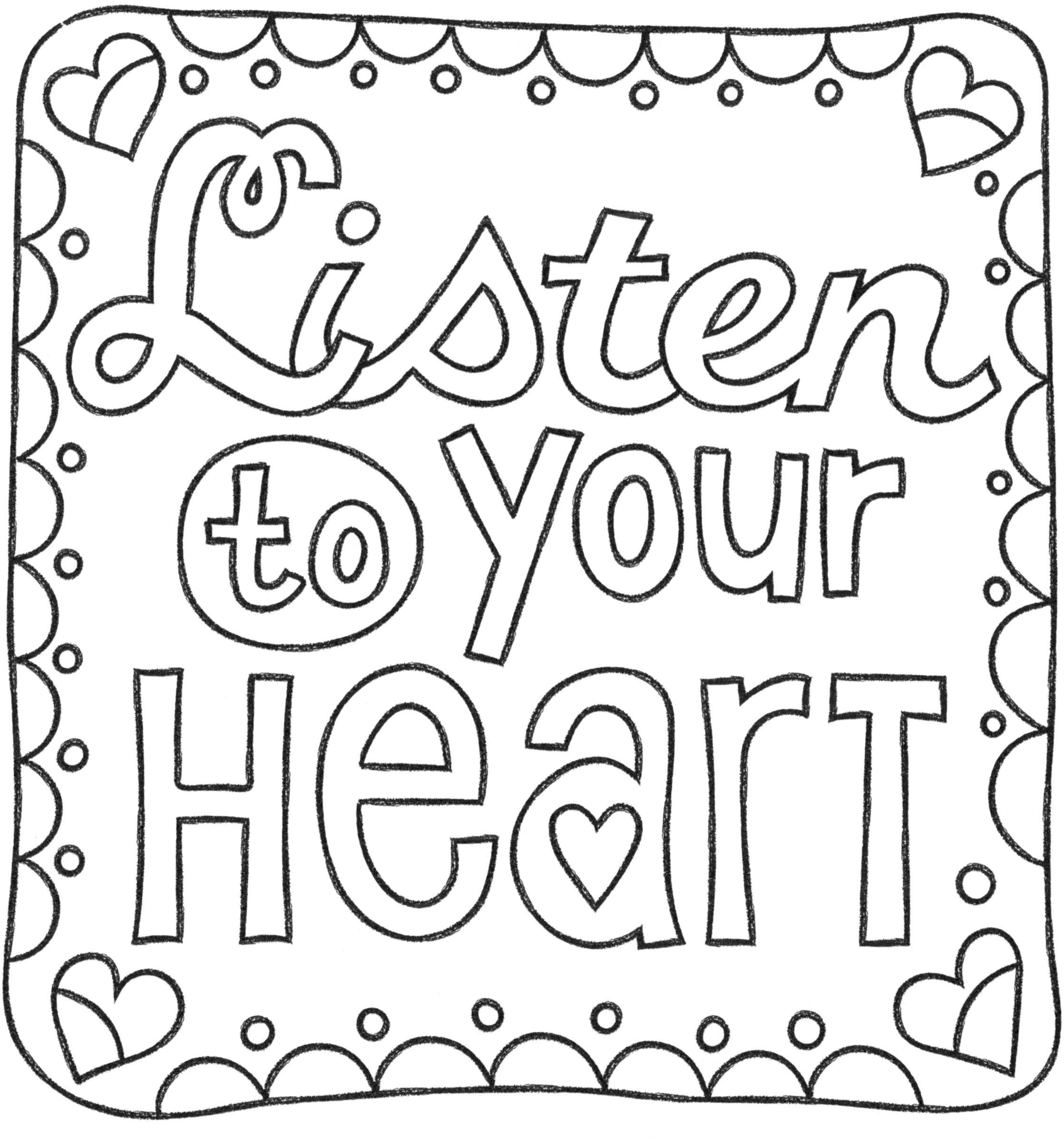
Listen
to your
Heart

Somewhere

I can do HARD things

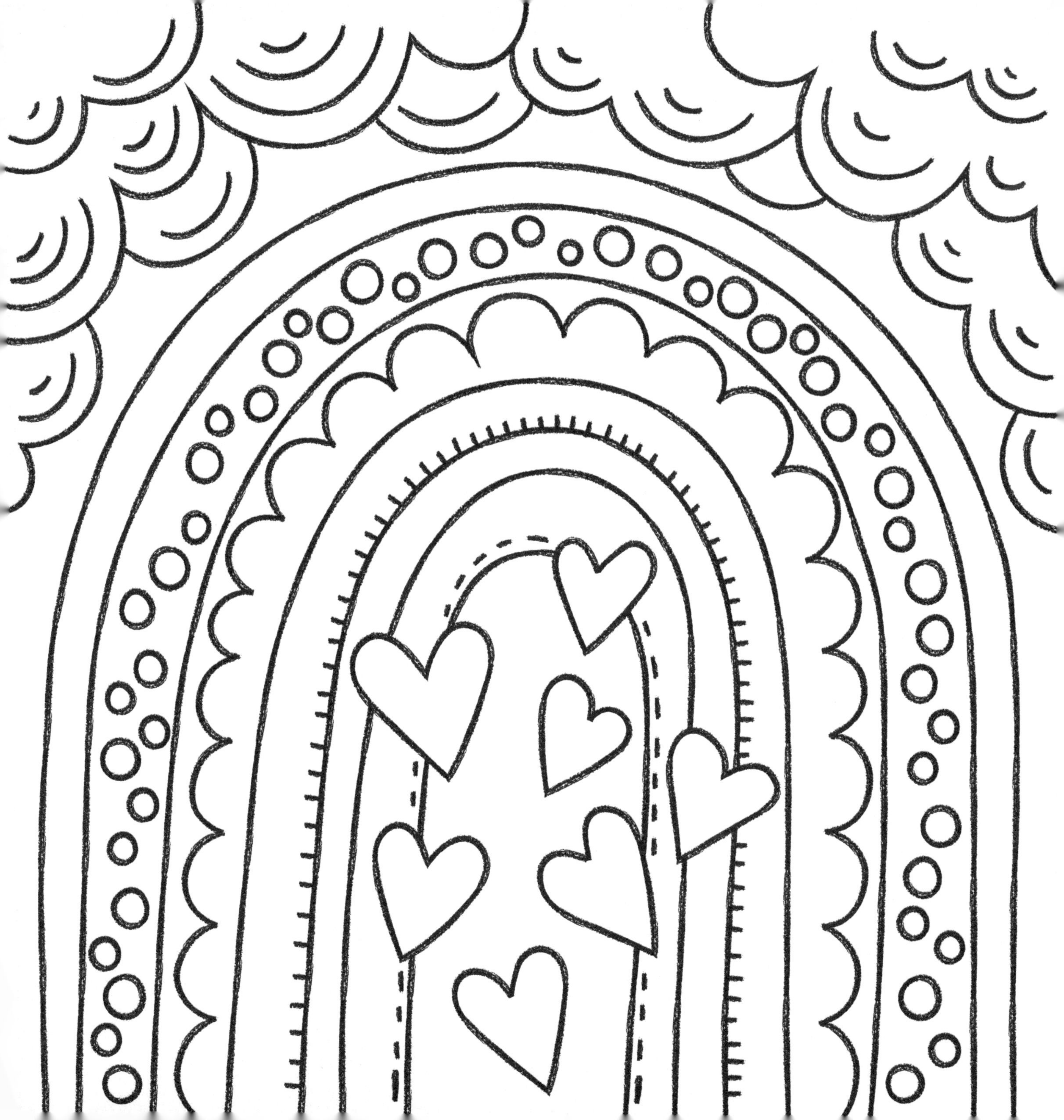

imagine create inspire

BE YOUTIFUL

Start WHERE YOU are

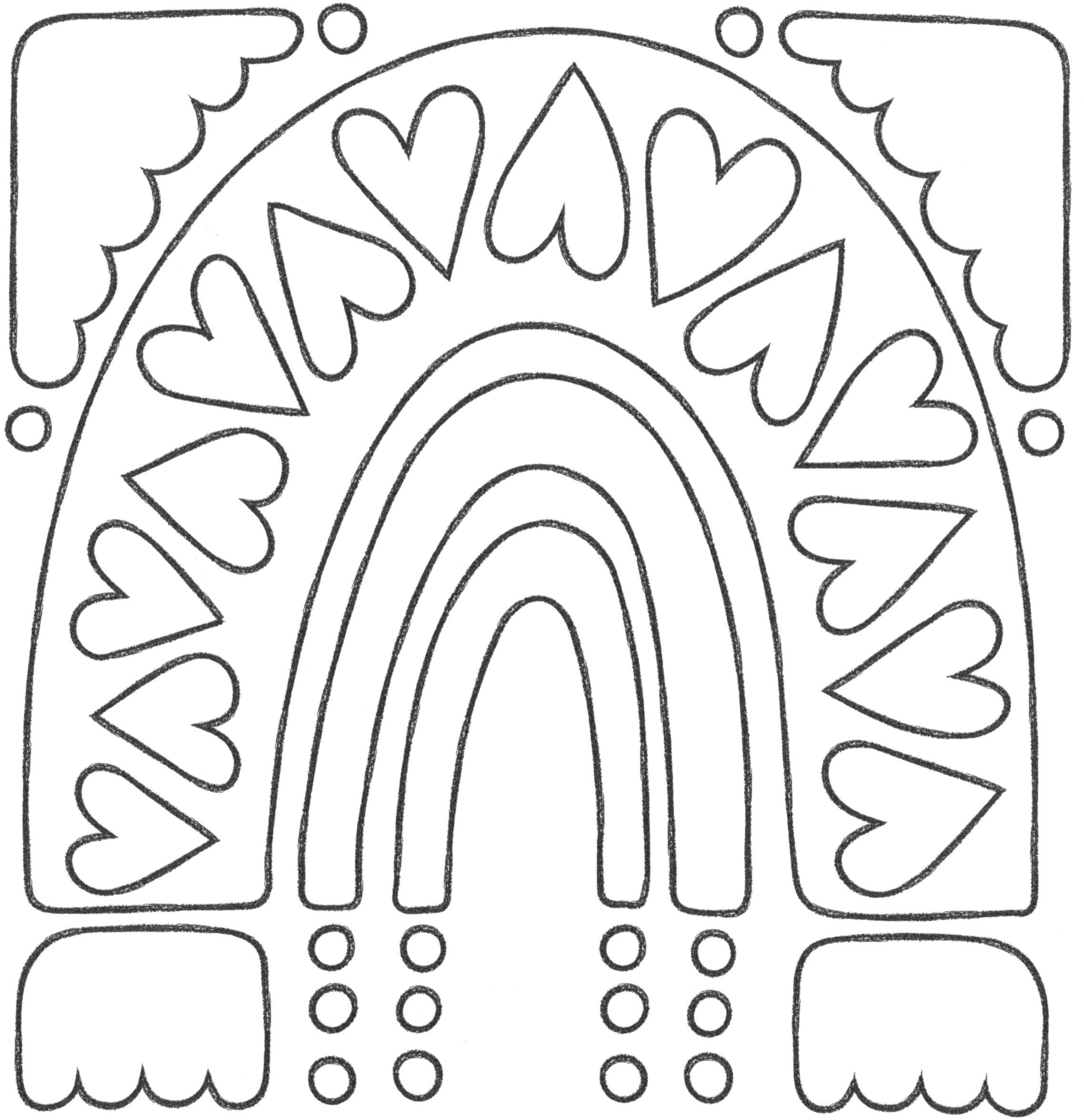

YES YOU CAN!

be a rainbow in someone else's cloud

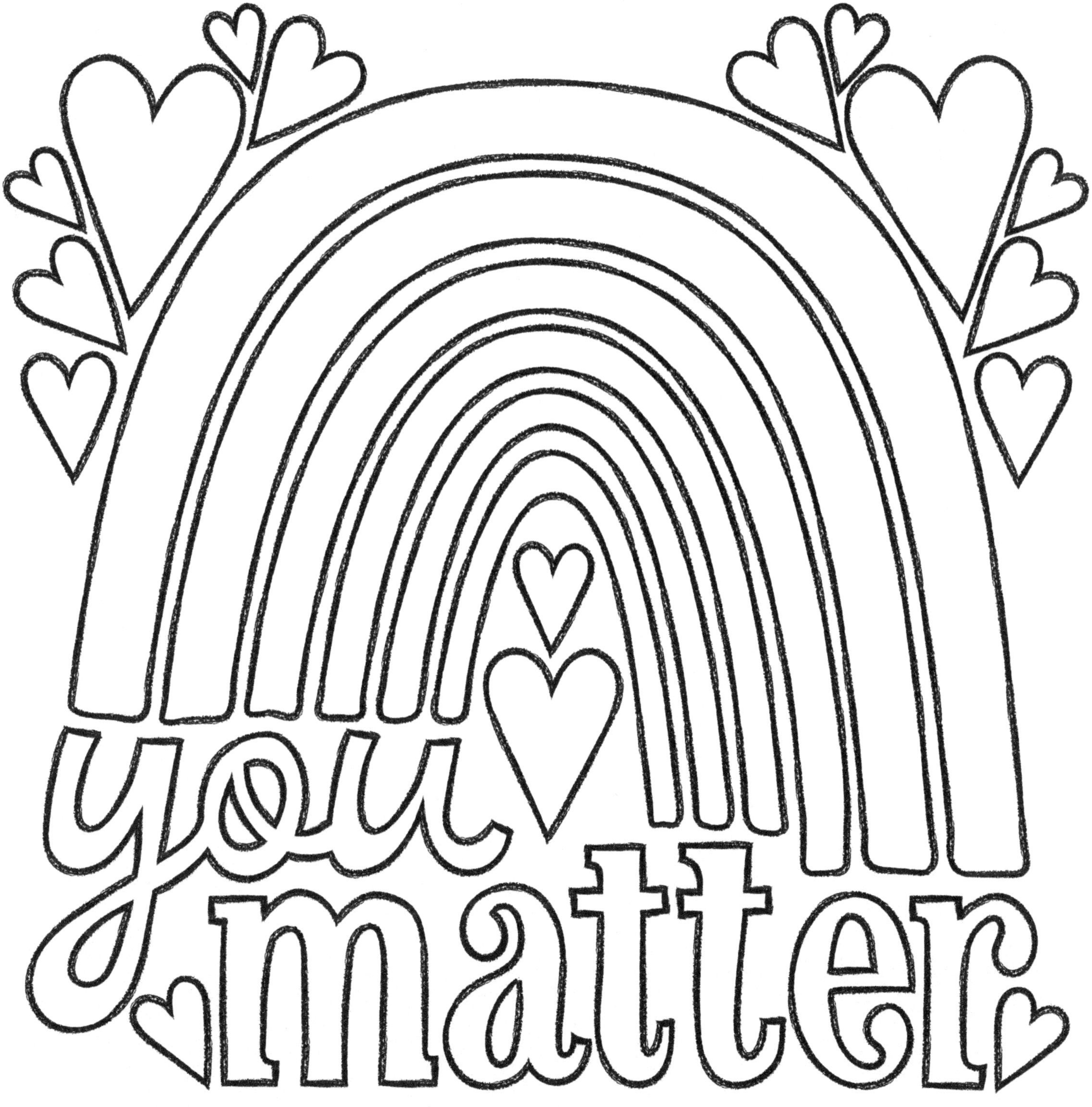
you
matter

POT O' LOVE

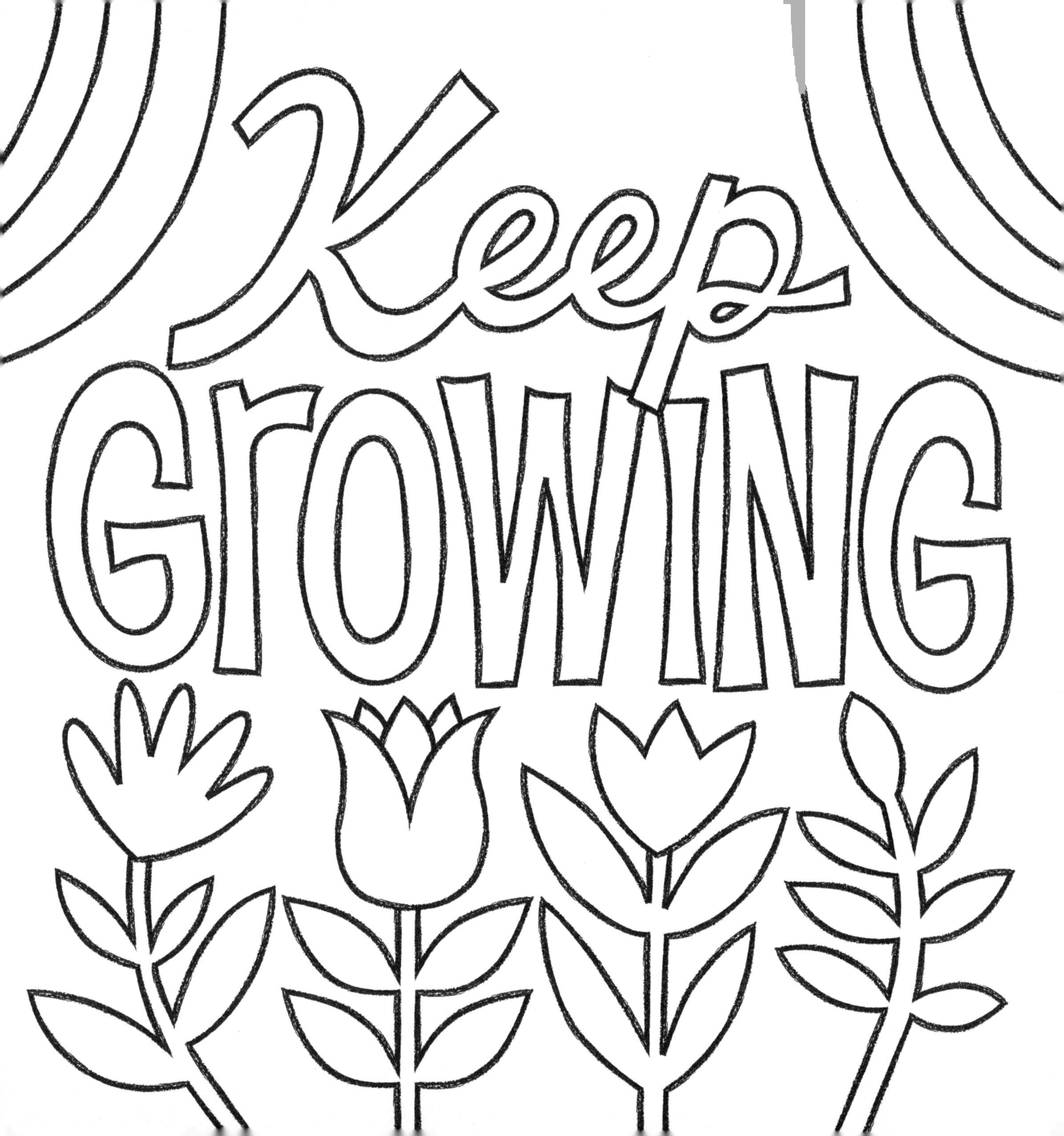
Keep
GROWING

Magic is here

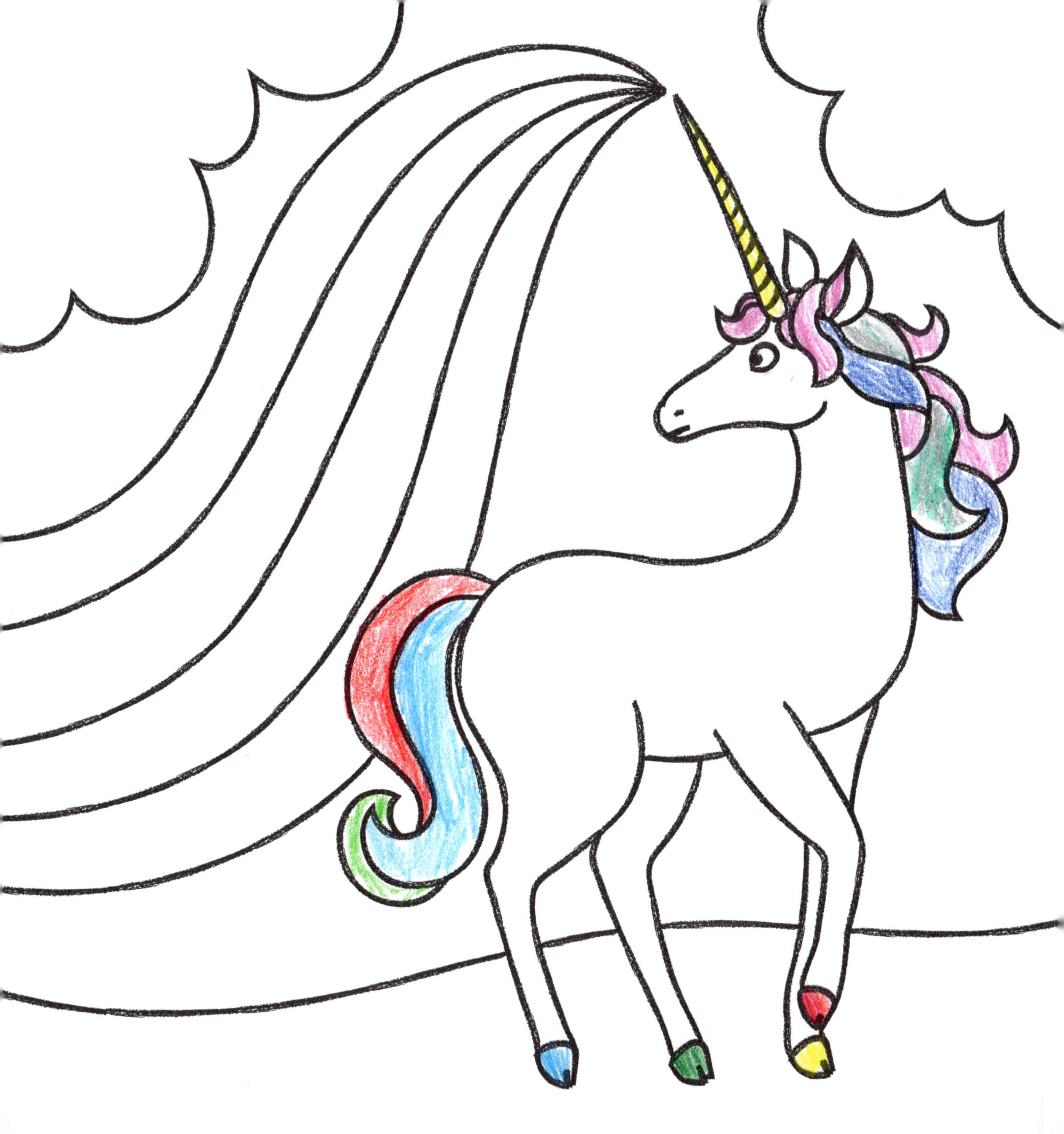

look at HOW FAR you've come

YOU ARE magic

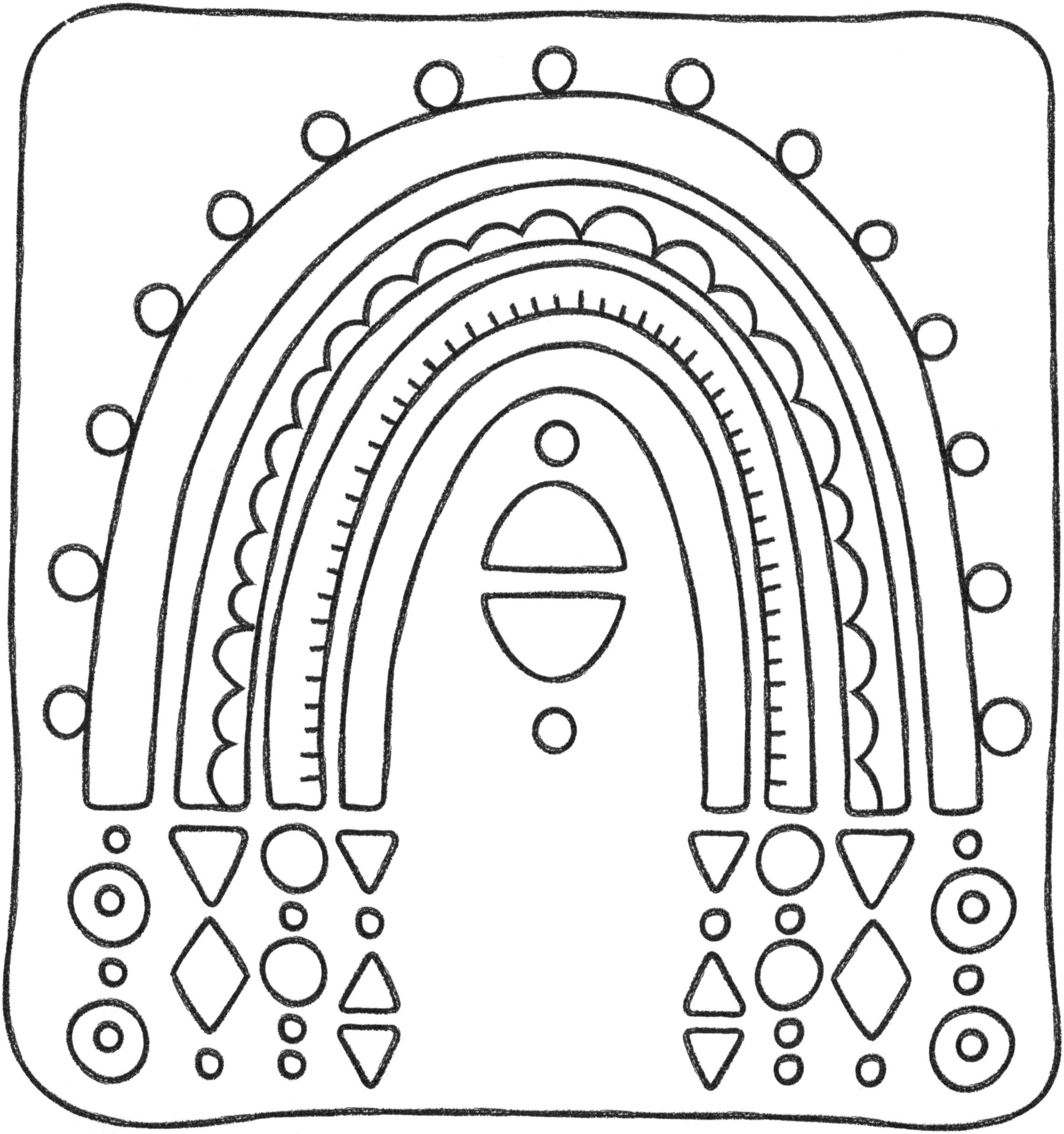

Treat Yourself With Kindness

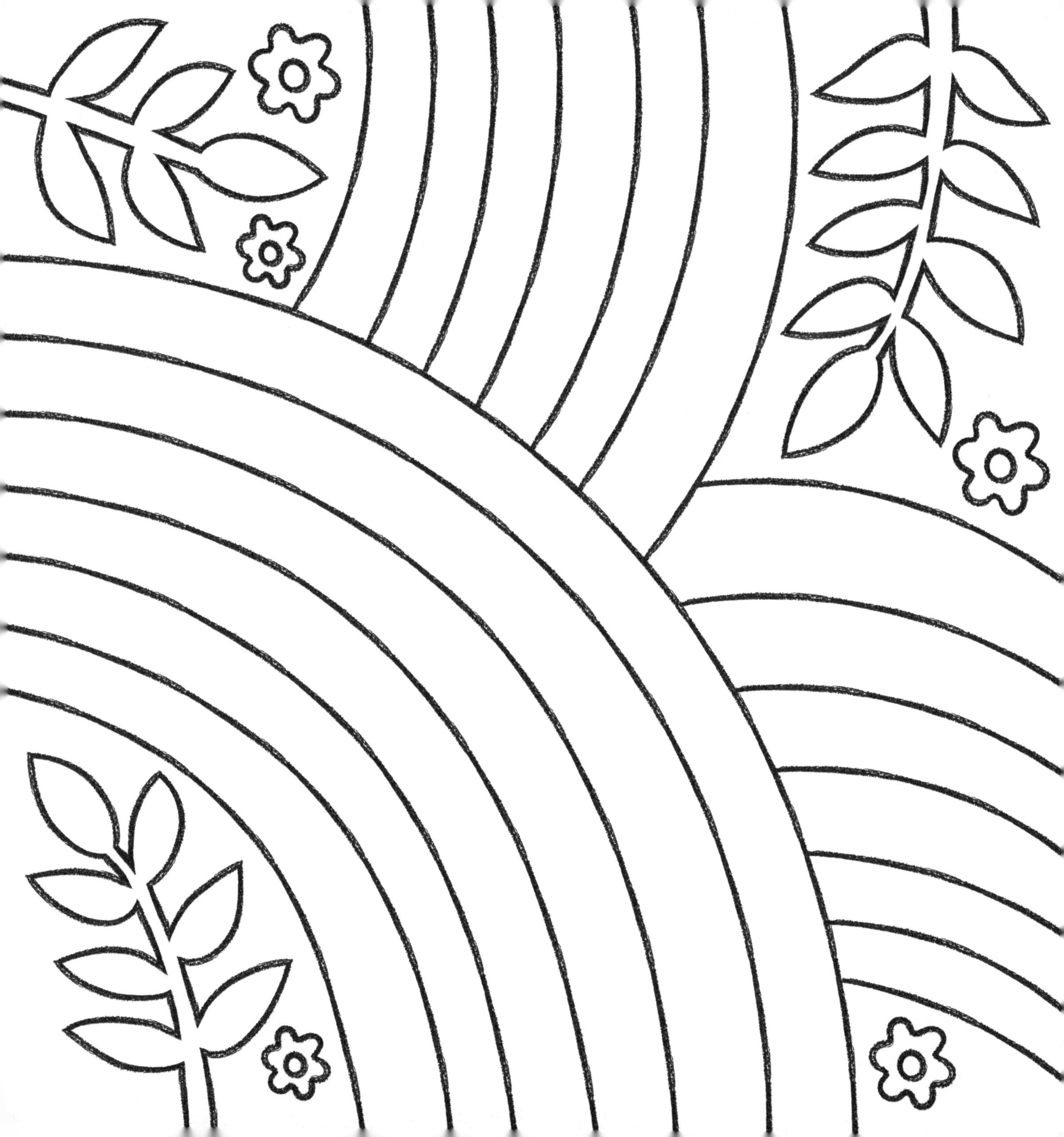

It'll All Work Out

good THINGS TAKE time

Help each other

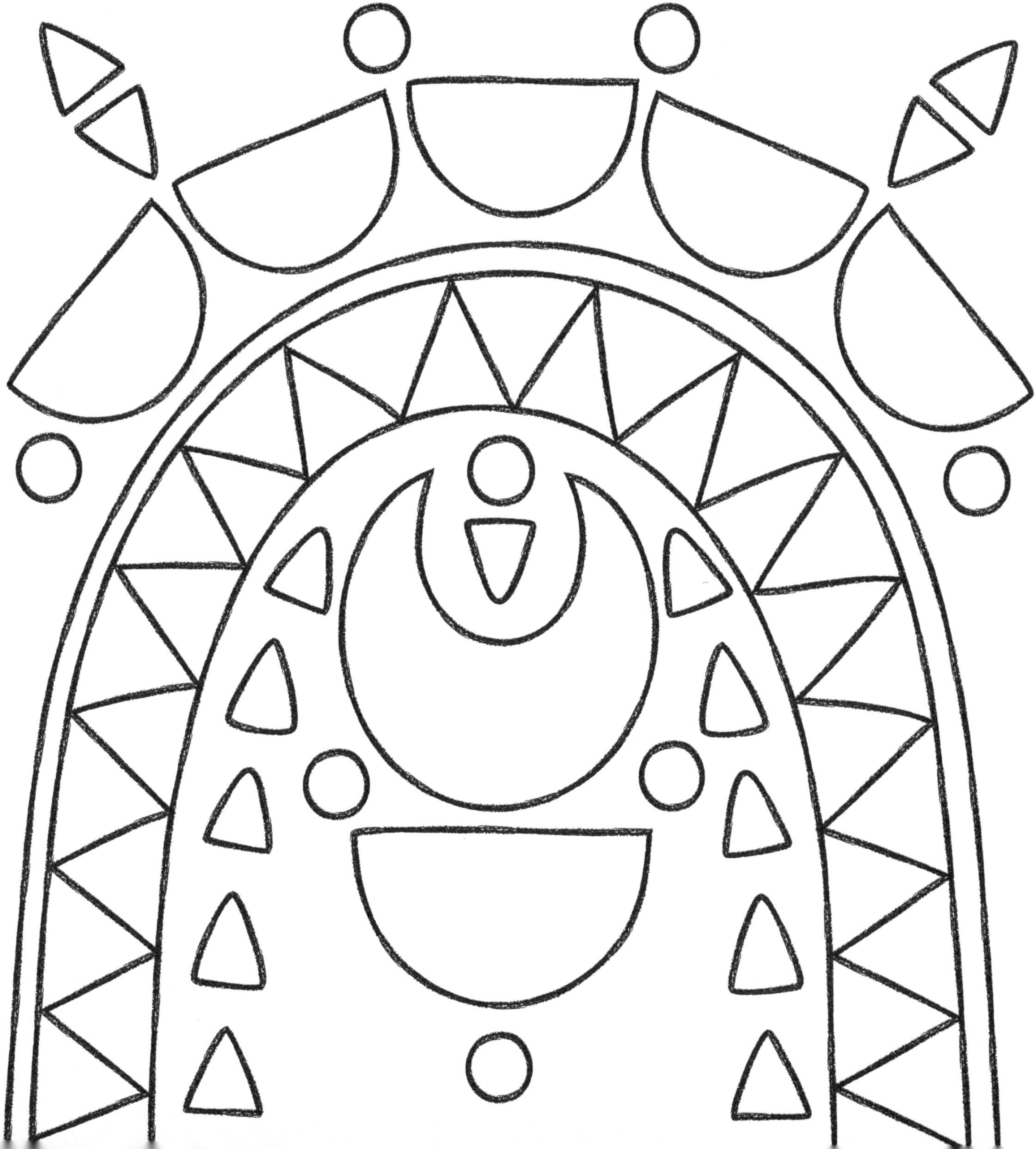

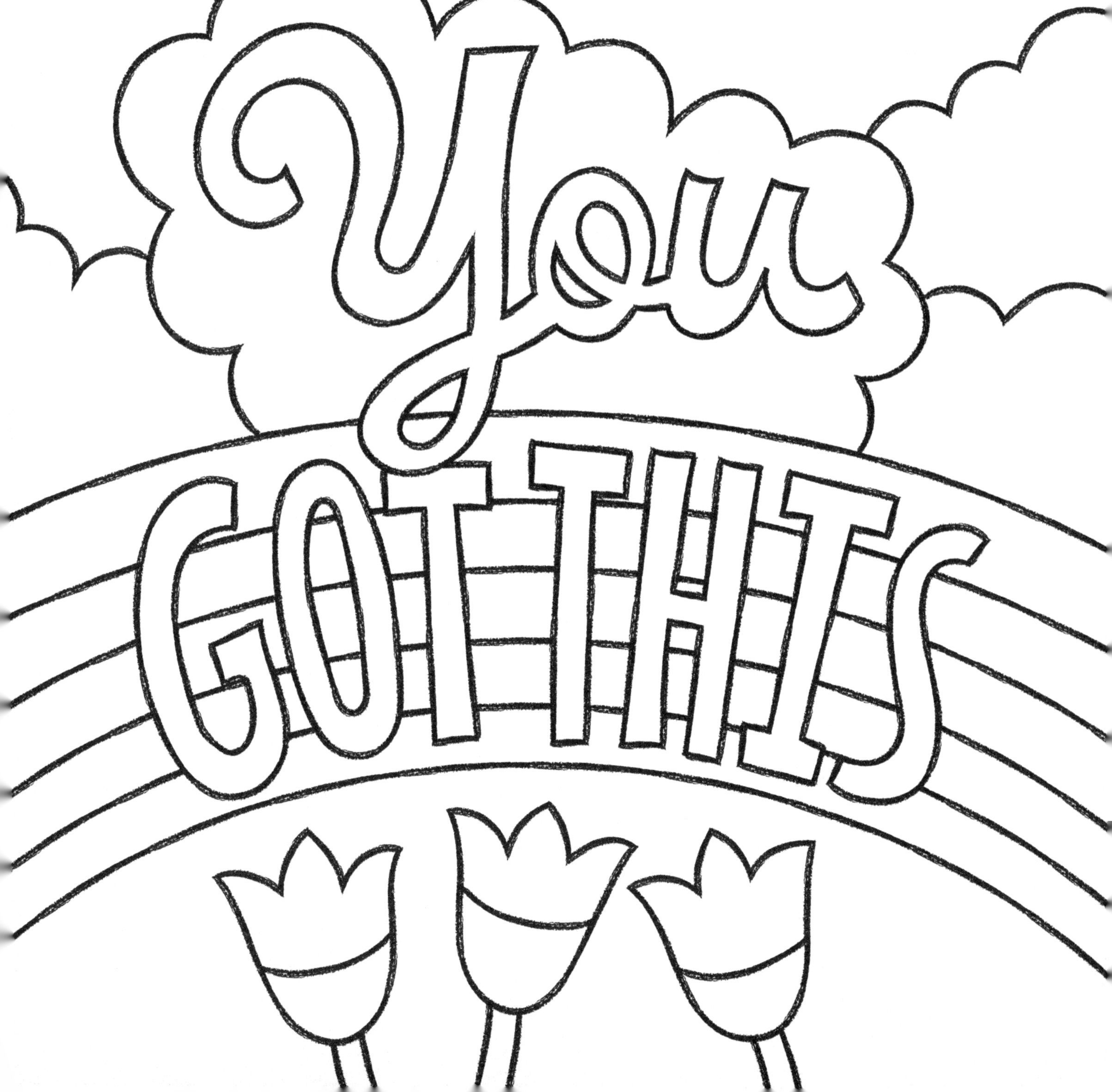
You
GOT THIS

One DAY at a TiME

Look for the helpers.

mr rogers

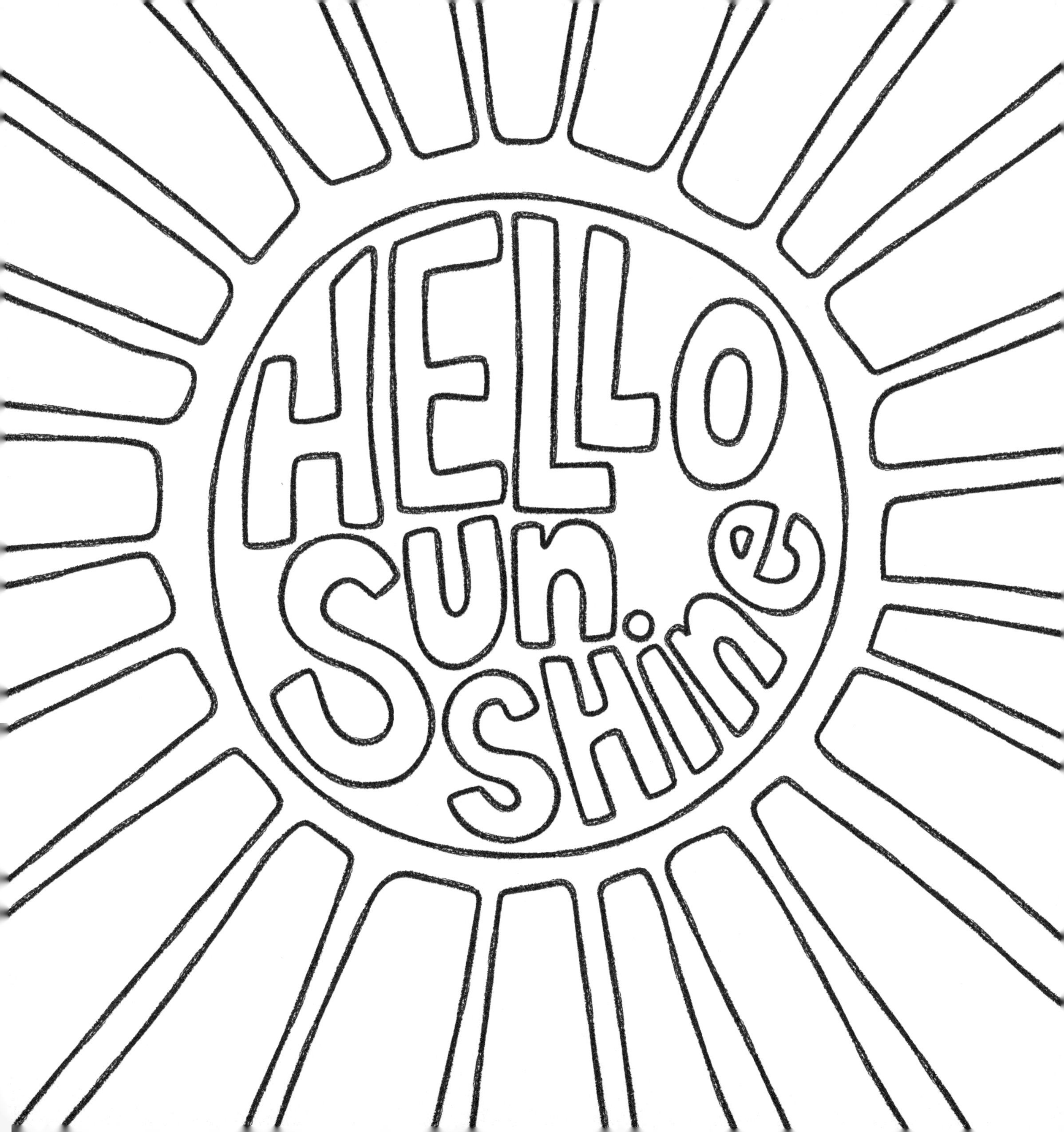
HELLO
Sun
Shine

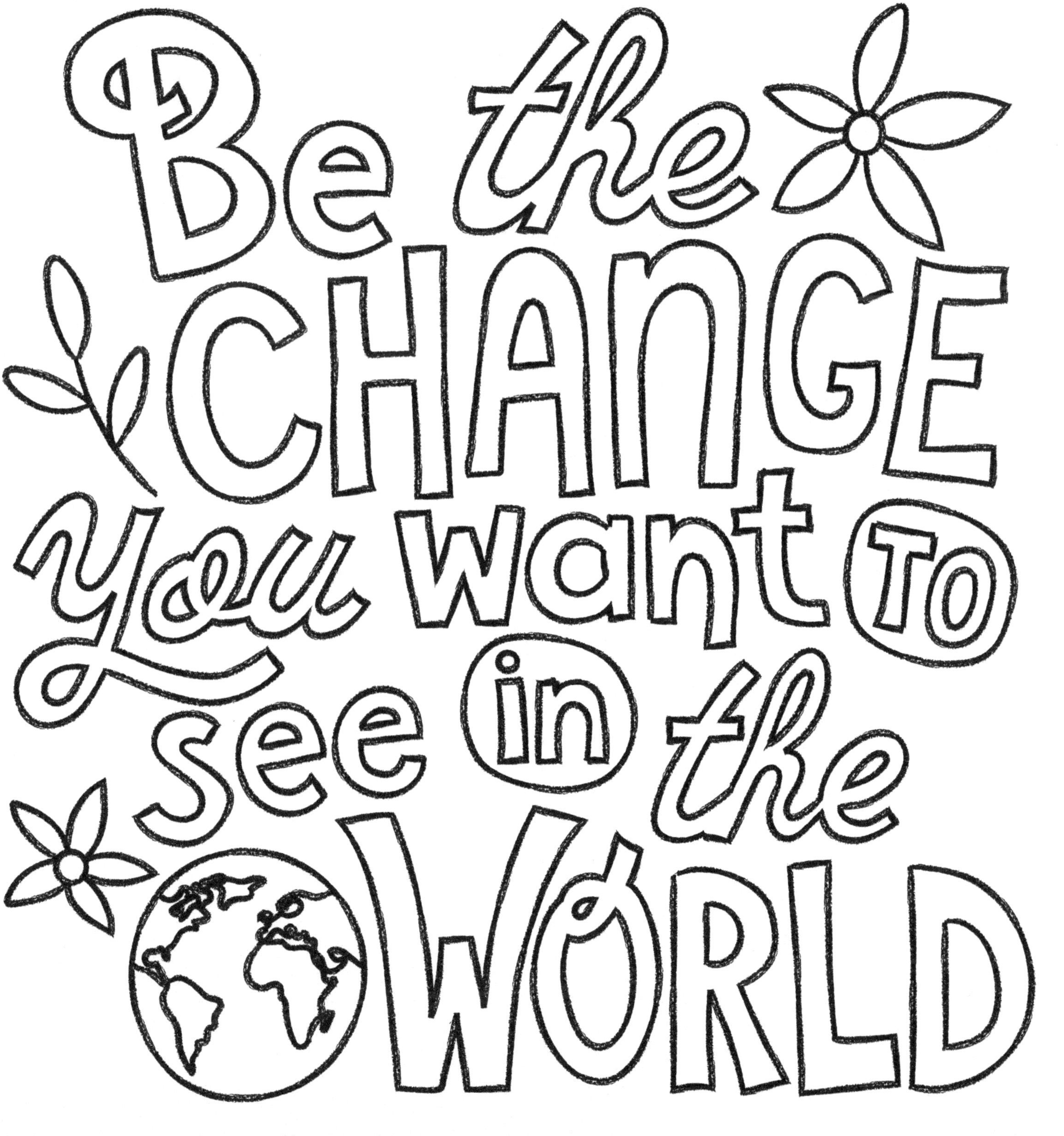
Be the
CHANGE
you want TO
see in the
WORLD

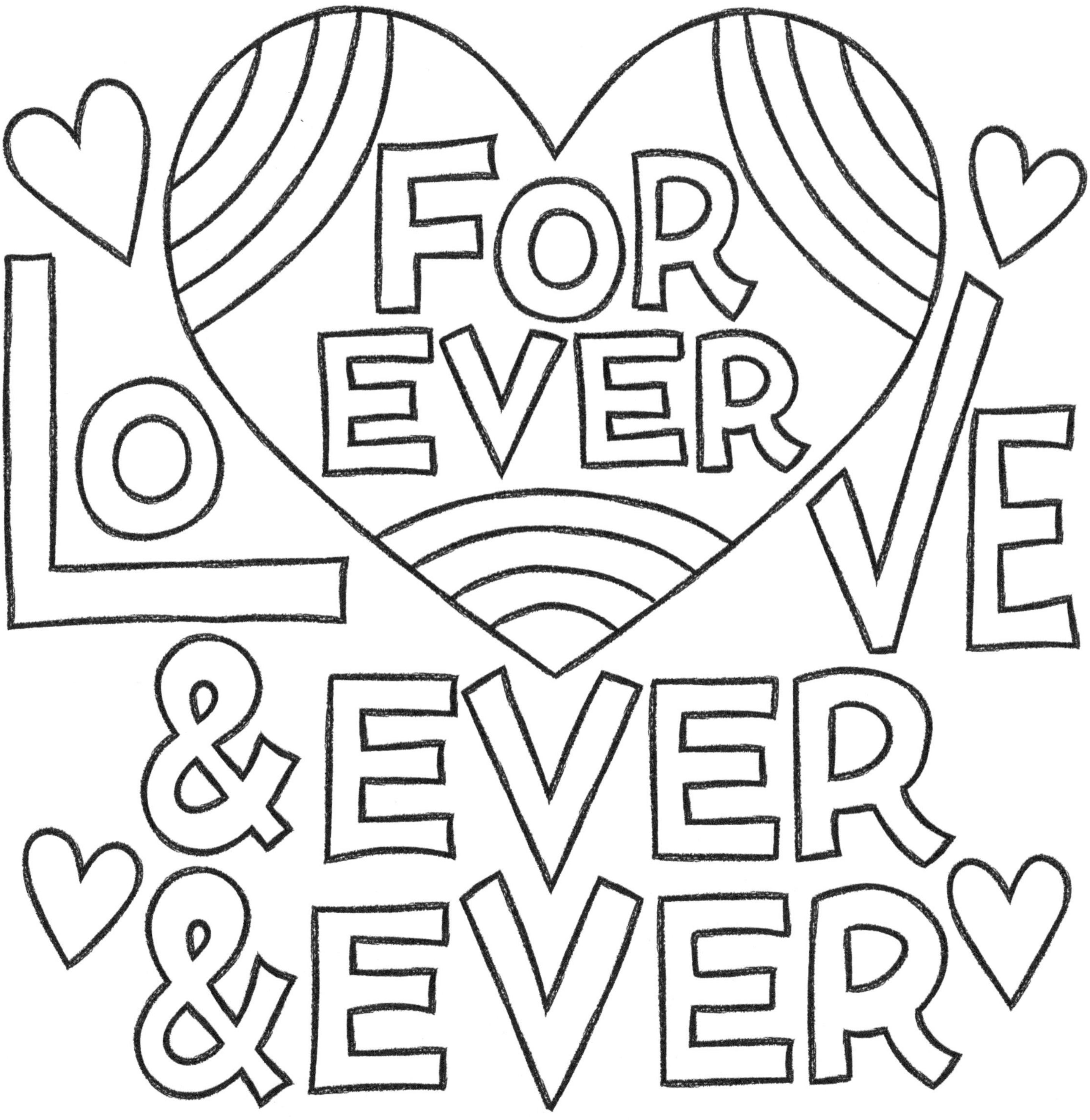
FOR
EVER
LO VE
& EVER
& EVER

We All Have Our Own Story

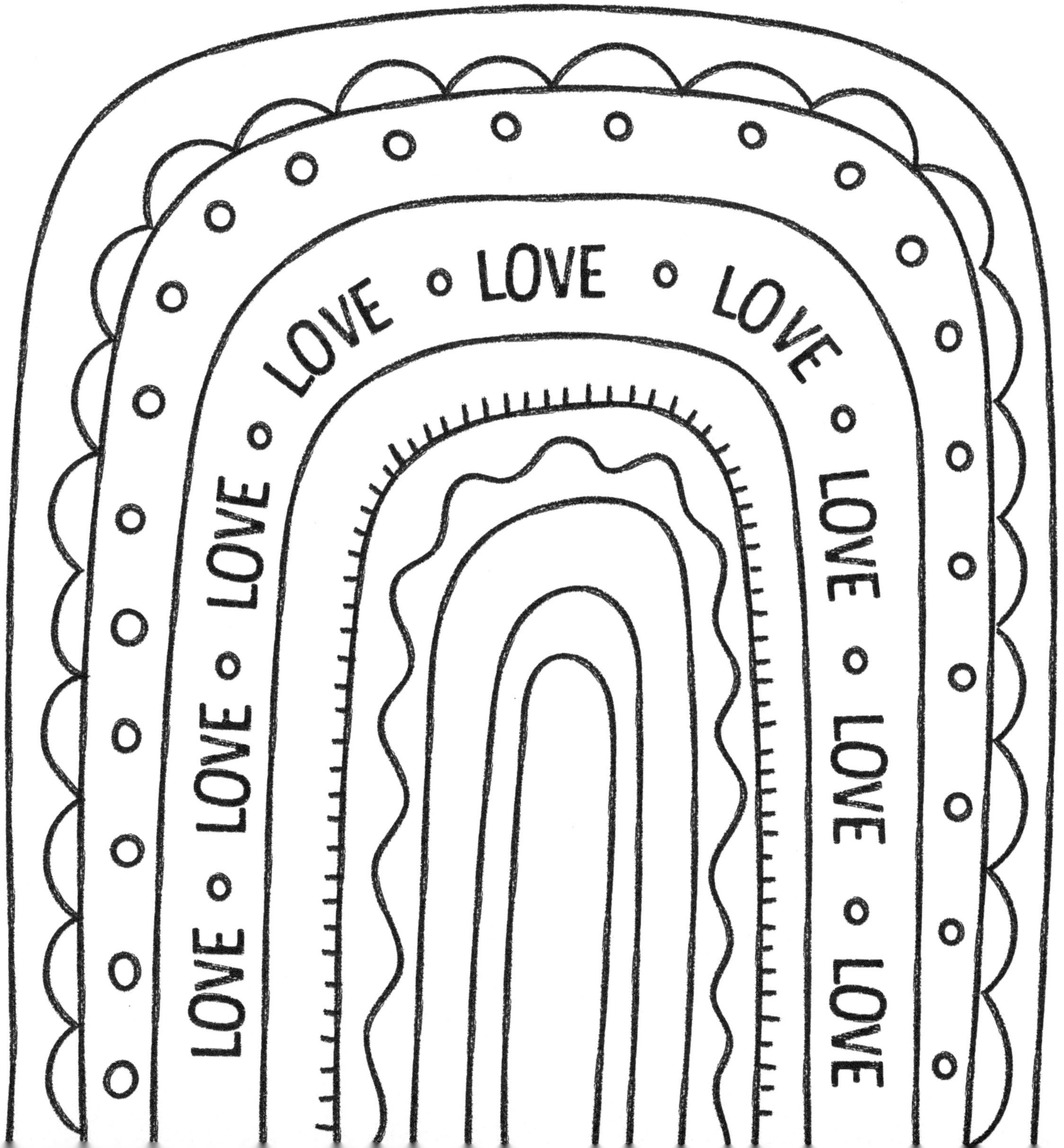
LOVE
LOVE
LOVE
LOVE
LOVE
LOVE
LOVE
LOVE
LOVE

NEVER STOP CHASING RAINBOWS

rest RESTORE grow

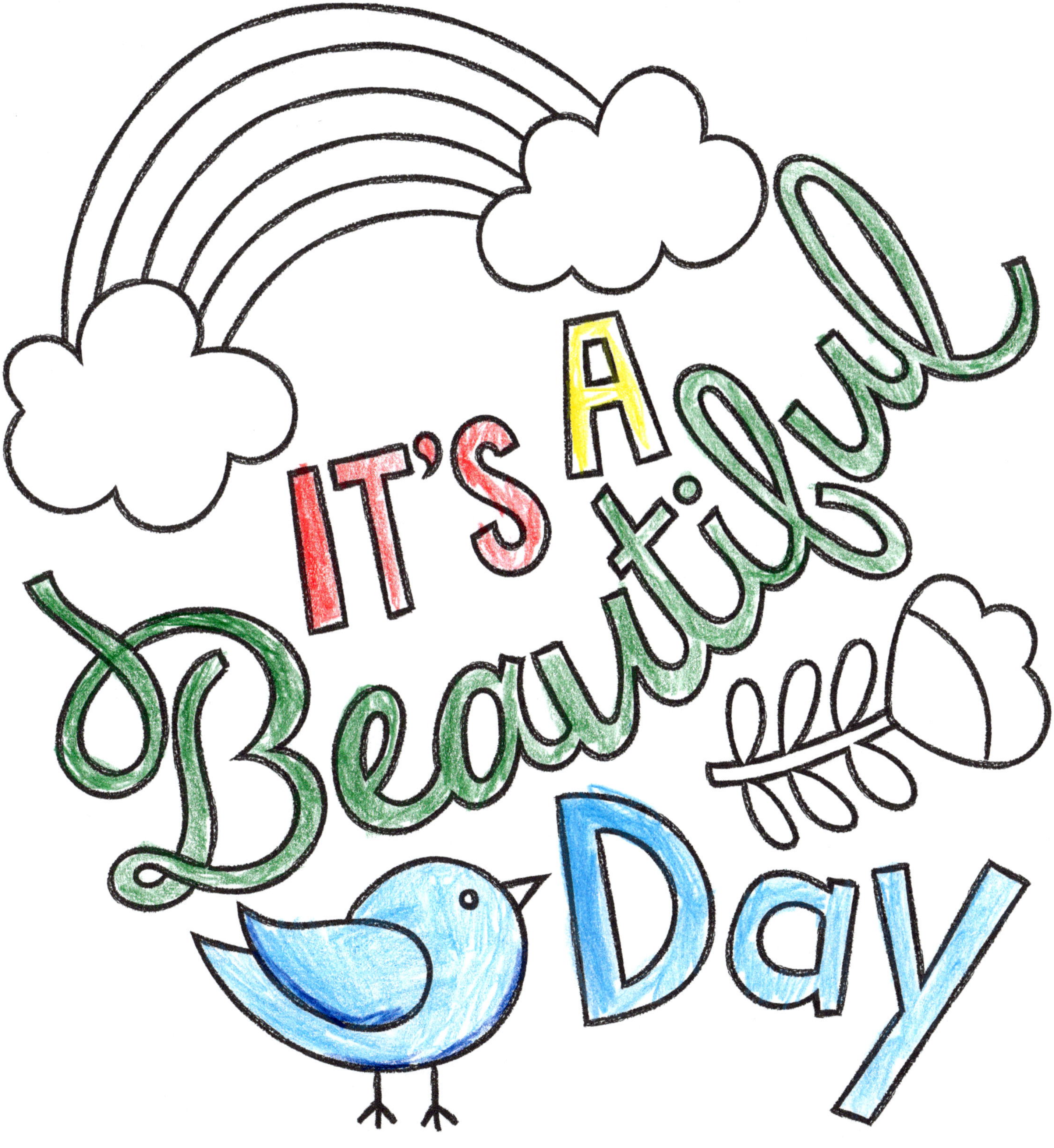
IT'S A Beautiful Day

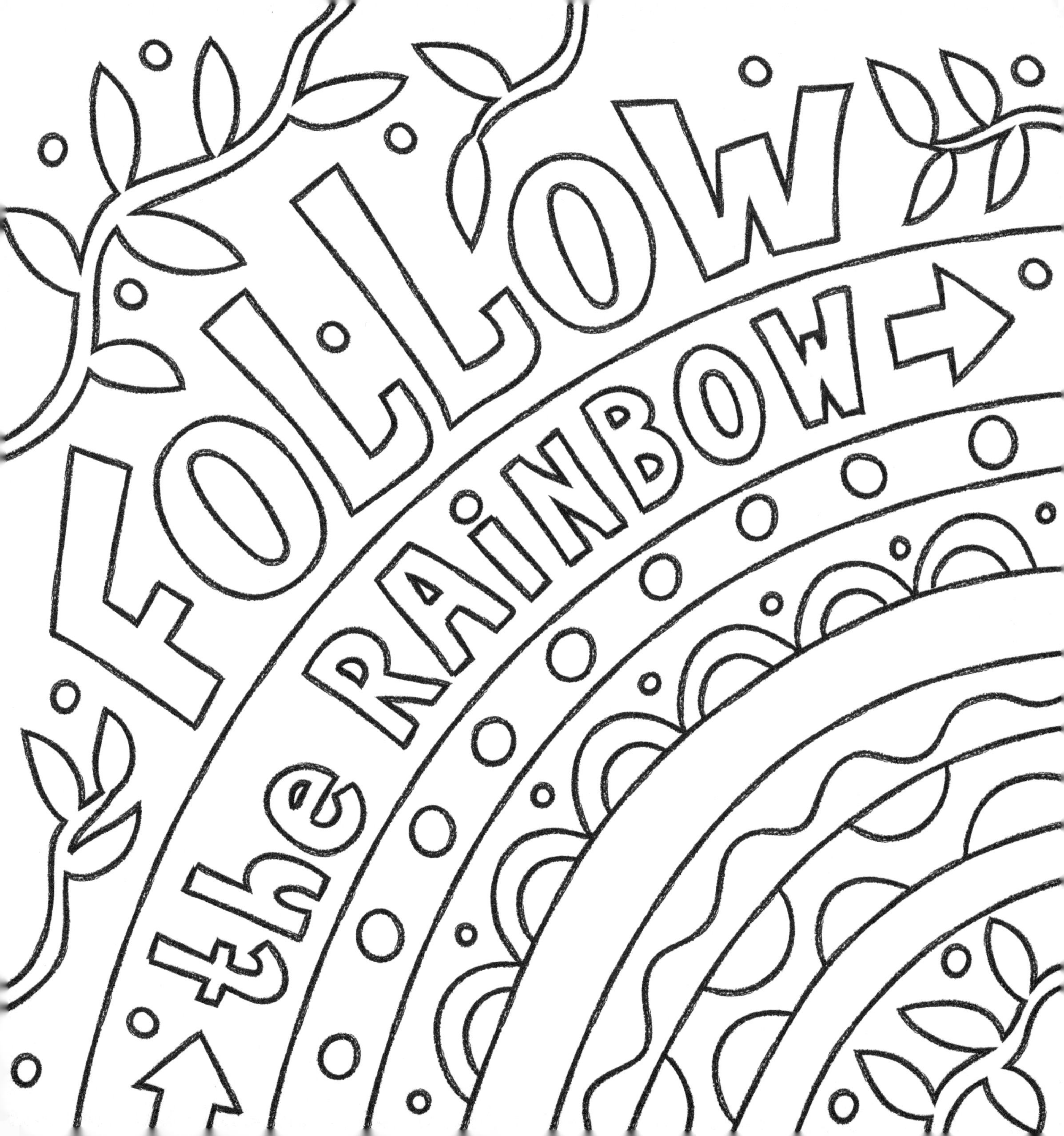

FOLLOW
the RAINBOW

You make TODAY BETTER

Progress Not Perfection

Let HOPE Win

Keep Going

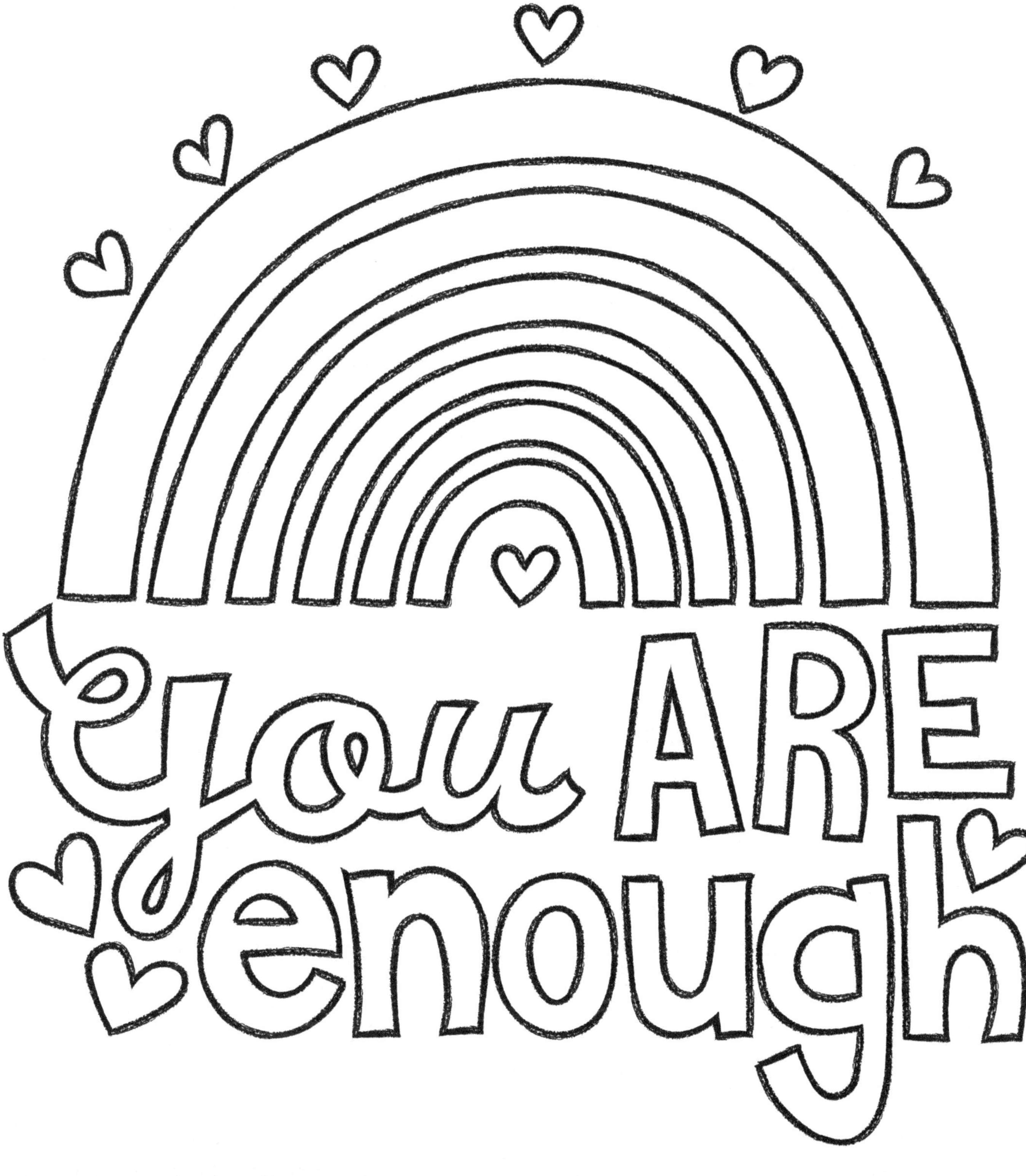
You ARE
enough

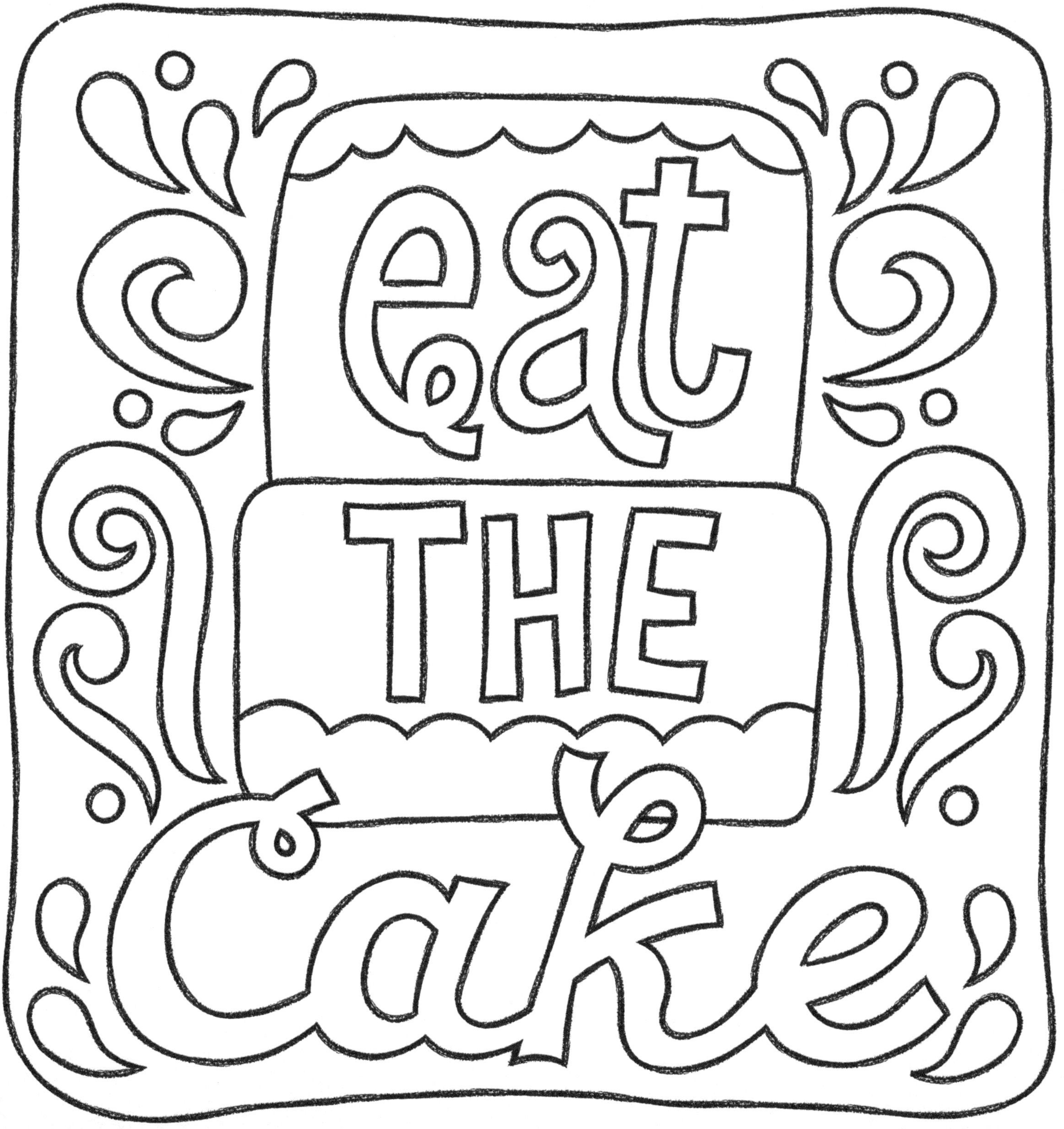
eat
THE
cake

Made in the USA
Middletown, DE
26 November 2021